THE BRAIN

X-TRAIN YOUR BRAIN

LEVEL **3**: INCREASING STAMINA

PUTTING YOUR LEFT AND RIGHT BRAIN TO THE TEST TO ENHANCE ALERTNESS AND MENTAL AGILITY

CORINNE L. GEDIMAN WITH FRANCIS M. CRINELLA, PH.D.

SELLERS
PUBLISHING

DEDICATION

To the memory of Harry Lille
— *Corinne L. Gediman*

Published by Sellers Publishing, Inc.
Copyright © 2013 Sellers Publishing Inc.
Text and puzzles copyright © 2013 Corinne L. Gediman
All rights reserved.

Sellers Publishing, Inc.
161 John Roberts Road, South Portland, Maine 04106
Visit our Web site: www.sellerspublishing.com
E-mail: rsp@rsvp.com

ISBN 13: 978-1-4162-0887-7

Designed by George Corsillo/Design Monsters

10 9 8 7 6 5 4 3 2 1

Printed and bound in the United States of America.

CONTENTS

LEVEL 3: INCREASING STAMINA

Welcome to the third level in *The Brain Works: X-Train Your Brain* series, created to get your brain back to peak performance by rejuvenating specific mental functions. The exercises in this volume are fun and engaging, and they present a moderate degree of challenge. This is the "increasing stamina" phase of your brain-exercise program. As you advance through the exercise levels, you will build increased brain stamina and enhance your mental agility. Each level brings you closer to a brighter and healthier brain. As in Levels 1 and 2, the exercises are a mix of left-brain (verbal), right-brain (visual-spatial), and whole-brain (left- and right-brain) workouts. You will see some familiar exercise formats as well as many new exercise types. Now that your brain has woken up and warmed up, you are ready for new brain challenges at a slightly higher level of mental stretch.

Level 3 is the third in a series of brain exercise workouts designed to help you build a better brain. Each level builds on the previous one, bringing you closer to a brighter and healthier brain. A new cognitive stretch in Level 3 is *processing speed*, which is the speed at which your brain processes information and makes connections. Processing speed slows naturally as we age, but it can be improved through practice and repetition. The puzzles in this book that offer opportunities to test and improve processing speed will be designated as such. In the processing-speed puzzles, your goal is to complete the last set of puzzles in a shorter time than it took you to complete the first set.

Note: If you participated in Level 1 or 2, it is not necessary to read the entire introduction again. However, if you did not participate in Level 1 or 2, it is highly recommended that you read the following information, as it provides the rationale and framework for your brain-fitness workout. The Brain-Dominance Self-Assessment in this volume is different from the one in Levels 1 and 2. It is recommended that all readers take this assessment prior to beginning the Level 3 exercises.

USE IT OR LOSE IT!

Whether you are a busy professional, a multitasking soccer mom, or a retiree, your quality of life depends on the health and resilience of your brain. Using new brain-imaging technology, neuroscientists can see that brain aging begins in our early twenties and that memory peaks at around age thirty. While this is disturbing news, there is a bright side, and our fate is not sealed.

The last decade has brought a wealth of knowledge about the brain and how it works. Perhaps the most amazing revelation is the brain's miraculous regenerative powers, known as neural plasticity. While once it was believed that brain aging was inevitable, it is now certain that exercising your brain by presenting it with novelty and mental challenges can help ward off mental decline and result in a brighter and healthier brain throughout your lifetime.

Without mental stimulation, however, brain cells slowly atrophy and die, much like body muscles that goes unused. When presented with mental challenges, brain cells light up and axons (nerve fibers) start firing. This electrical-chemical activity gets brain cells "talking" to each. It is this "chatter" that leads to new communication pathways and stronger neuronal connections between brain cells. The result is a healthier, more resilient brain capable of delaying and even warding off dementia and other diseases of the brain. And the best part is that building a brawnier brain is a lifestyle choice.

EXERCISE FOR A BETTER BRAIN

X-Train Your Brain is a brain-exercise program designed by experts in the field. It works on the proven principle that mental muscle, much like physical muscle, can be gained and maintained through an exercise regimen. The program parallels a physical workout routine at your gym, in which you begin by warming up unused muscles, progress to building core strength, and then increase your stamina and accelerate the pace.

There are four exercise levels contained in this series. Each level builds on the last and brings you closer to a better brain.

Level 1: Basic Warm-Up (Stress Free)
Level 2: Building Core Strength (Easy)
Level 3: Increasing Stamina (Moderate)
Level 4: Accelerating the Pace (More Challenging)

X-TRAIN EXERCISE GOAL

Just as a sedentary lifestyle won't keep your body in peak physical condition, a sedentary brain won't retain its mental edge. Retaining peak mental performance is the key to reversing the mental deficits associated with an aging brain, including memory loss, sluggish thinking, and problem-solving confusion. It is much easier to maintain mental abilities than to try to regain them, in the same way that it is easier to maintain muscle tone than to try and regain it. A successful exercise program needs to be *comprehensive, confidence building*, and *fun*. *X-Train Your Brain: Level 3* is designed to meet all three of these criteria.

COMPREHENSIVE

Athletes achieve peak physical performance through cross-training, and we apply this same method for brain athletes. Cross-training your brain makes perfect sense, given the brain's own natural anatomy. The two hemispheres of the cerebral cortex (gray matter) are divided right down the middle into a left hemisphere and a right hemisphere. Each side of the brain is specialized and shows dominance with regard to specific mental processes and abilities. The "left brain" excels at verbal abilities, logic, and linear problem solving, while the "right brain" is adept at visual perception, spatial relationships, and creative problem solving. Collectively these abilities contribute to a fully functioning whole brain. *X-Train Your Brain* targets both left- and right-brain functions and mental abilities, for a comprehensive and total-brain workout.

CONFIDENCE BUILDING

X-Train Your Brain is designed to build confidence and demonstrate your gains. At the gym, progress is easy to see. While last month I was lifting 5-pound weights, this month I can lift 10-pound weights. When I started my workout program, I was doing 15 minutes on the treadmill; now I'm doing 45 minutes.

Level 3 of this series starts off with exercises and games that are fun and easily mastered. This ensures a satisfying, no-stress experience, allowing you to increase your mental stamina at a comfortable, relaxed pace. As you move forward you'll gain the confidence and skills to take on greater challenges. To facilitate success, all of the exercises are preceded by "how to" instructions and examples, so that you know exactly how to approach each puzzle or game.

FUN

Sticking with an exercise program is not easy, as evidenced by lapsed gym memberships and retired exercise equipment sitting in basements. Despite good intentions, physical exercise can become routine, time-consuming, and somewhat boring. That's why only highly motivated, type A personalities tend to stick with it over time.

It's essential to avoid these same pitfalls in a brain-exercise program. The *X-Train Your Brain* series is anything but routine, boring, or time-consuming. Every exercise brings novelty and a new, intriguing mental challenge. Exercises are structured as games and puzzles to ensure a fun and enjoyable workout. And you set your own pace. Success isn't determined by how many exercises you do in a sitting, or how many you get right. Success means bringing some mental challenge and novelty to your brain every day to keep it sharp and agile. The goal is a better quality of mental life.

Since many of the exercises are set up like games, they can be enjoyed by more than one person, or even by competing teams. The processing-speed element in this volume will help you turn an exercise into a friendly game: the winner is the player or team that is able to increase speed the most between puzzles of the same type. Adding timed play to the challenge helps you work on your mental-processing speed, which slows down with age.

BRAIN DOMINANCE

Before you get started, it's interesting to know which side of your brain is dominant. Brain dominance relates to specific mental functions and thinking styles. Most people have a preferred brain-dominance orientation. Your brain dominance will create an affinity for and ease with some puzzles over others. If you are left-brain dominant, you'll definitely enjoy the word games but may struggle with the visual puzzles, and vice versa. You may even be tempted to stick with the exercises that match your brain dominance and skip those that do not. But that would defeat the purpose of a cross-training program, and your gains would be minimized. Remember, the more a mental workout takes you out of your comfort zone, the more novelty it brings to your brain. And the greatest gains come with novelty, because new brain pathways are being tapped.

LEFT-BRAIN CHARACTERISTICS

The left side of the brain excels at language skills, verbal processing, sequential reasoning, and analytical thinking. Individuals who favor this type of thinking are said to be left-brain dominant. They are characterized as logical and rational thinkers capable of excelling in many fields, including science, mathematics, writing, accounting, financial services, teaching, medicine, engineering, research, library science, and computer programming. When problem solving, left-brain-dominant thinkers arrive at the solution or big picture by analyzing and organizing the step-by-step details along the way. They are good forward planners and usually enjoy "talking out" a problem. This brain orientation is compatible with traditional classroom learning, in which students are rewarded for finding the "right" answer.

RIGHT-BRAIN CHARACTERISTICS

The right side of the brain shows dominance in visual-spatial reasoning, random processing (i.e., free association), intuition, perceptual organization, and holistic thinking. Holistic thinkers are able to "see" the "whole" as a picture. They retain information through the use of images and patterns. Perceptual organization, a right-brain-dominant strength, is the process by which the brain takes bits and pieces of visual information (color, lines, shapes) and structures the individual parts into larger units and interrelationships. Individuals who excel in perceptual organization show an ability to arrange color, lines, and shapes into creative works of art, sculpture, and architecture. In school, right-brain-dominant children are whizzes at solving visual challenges, such as puzzles, mazes, block building, hidden blocks, and visual mathematical patterns. In fact, they may be brilliant mathematicians who easily grasp geometry and physics, but be poor calculators who struggle to grasp the linear logic in algebra. Some occupations that attract a right-brain person are inventor, architect, forest ranger, illustrator, artist, actor, athlete, interior decorator, beautician, mathematician, computer-graphics designer, craftsperson, photographer, recreation director, marketing designer, retail specialist, yoga/dance instructor, art director, Web-site designer, fashion designer, and product-package designer.

BRAIN-DOMINANCE SELF-ASSESSMENT

The Brain-Dominance Self-Assessment below will provide insight into whether you are naturally left-brain or right-brain dominant. It will help you understand where your mental strengths lie, as well as what your greatest "mental stretch" opportunities are.

For each item, circle the letter "a" or "b" beside the answer that most closely describes your preference. You must choose either "a" or "b" — you cannot choose both. If you are not sure, consider what your response would be if you were in a stressful, difficult, or new situation. We tend to revert to our natural brain dominance when under pressure.

1 I am often late getting places.
       a. yes
       b. no

2 When you are learning dance steps, it is easier for you to . . .
       a. learn by imitation and by getting the feel of the music.
       b. learn the sequence of movements and talk yourself through it.

3 If I don't know which way to turn, I usually let my emotions lead me.
       a. yes
       b. no

4 Can you tell approximately how much time has passed without a watch?
       a. yes
       b. no

5 I find that sticking to a schedule is boring.
       a. yes
       b. no

6 If I lost something, I would visualize where I last saw it.
       a. yes
       b. no

7 Setting goals for myself helps me to keep from slacking off.
       a. yes
       b. no

8 When I work, I tend to . . .
       a. focus on one task at a time.
       b. multitask; have a bunch of projects going at the same time.

9 I feel most comfortable when there is a specific set of directions to follow.

     a. yes
     b. no

10 Does the expression "Life is just a bowl of cherries" make sense to you?

     a. yes
     b. no

11 I am musically inclined.

     a. yes
     b. no

12 My desk, work area, or laundry room is . . .

     a. cluttered with things I might need later.
     b. organized and neat.

13 Do you sometimes act spontaneously or come to premature conclusions?

     a. yes
     b. no

14 Some people think I'm psychic.

     a. yes
     b. no

15 When I need to learn how to use a new piece of equipment . . .

     a. I jump right in and wing it.
     b. I carefully read the instruction manual before beginning.

16 Are you a romantic dreamer or a logical planner?

     a. romantic dreamer
     b. logical planner

17 Before I take a stand on an issue, I get all the facts.

     a. yes
     b. no

18 I like to draw.

      a. yes

      b. no

19 I lose track of time easily.

      a. yes

      b. no

20 I feel comfortable expressing myself with words.

      a. yes

      b. no

21 If you forget someone's name, would you go through the alphabet until you remembered it?

      a. yes

      b. no

22 Have you considered being a poet, a politician, an architect, or a dancer?

      a. yes

      b. no

23 Have you considered becoming a lawyer, a journalist, or a doctor?

      a. yes

      b. no

24 I keep a "to do" list.

      a. yes

      b. no

25 Is it easy for you to categorize and put away files?

      a. yes

      b. no

Brain-Dominance Answer Key

If your answers to the questions above are fairly evenly distributed between left- and right-brain responses, you are a "whole brain" thinker with the flexibility to draw on the strengths of both brain hemispheres. If the majority of your responses fall into one or the other brain-hemisphere categories, your natural tendencies are to draw on the strengths of your primary brain dominance as you engage in everyday activities and challenges.

Left-Brain Responses: 1. b, 2. b, 3. b, 4. a, 5. b, 6. b, 7. a, 8. a, 9. a, 10. b, 11. b, 12. b, 13. b, 14. b, 15. b, 16. b, 17. a, 18. b, 19. b, 20. b, 21. a, 22. b, 23. a, 24. a, 25. a

Right-Brain Responses: 1. a, 2. a, 3. a, 4. b, 5. a, 6. a, 7. b, 8. b, 9. b, 10. a, 11. a, 12. a, 13. a, 14. a, 15. a, 16. a, 17. b, 18. a, 19. a, 20. a, 21. b, 22. a, 23. b, 24. b, 25. b

GETTING STARTED

You are now ready to begin your journey toward becoming a brain athlete! Remember that the key is to relax and have fun. Did you know that stress kills brain cells? So no stressing. You are about to do something really good for yourself. Enjoy it and feel proud.

PART 1:
LEFT BRAIN

CAN YOU SAY IT?

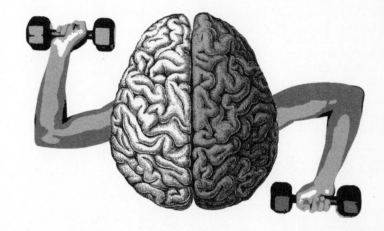

VERBAL EXERCISES

LEFT BRAIN: CAN YOU SAY IT? VERBAL EXERCISES

INTRODUCTION:

The focus of the left-brain exercises is on the left hemisphere's natural proclivity for language skills. Keeping language processing sharp as we age is critical to memory formation, storage, and retrieval. In this left-brain workout, you will participate in a variety of entertaining verbal exercises.

LEFT   RIGHT

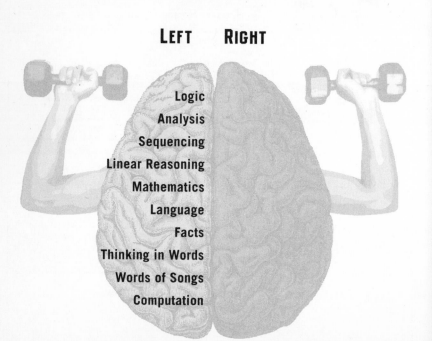

Logic
Analysis
Sequencing
Linear Reasoning
Mathematics
Language
Facts
Thinking in Words
Words of Songs
Computation

HOW TO PLAY:

Beheadment sounds like something horrible and gory, but it isn't. It's a form of word play. A beheadment is a word that produces another word when you chop off the first letter. Can you figure out the missing words in the beheadment below?

I saw a man _____ an old _____ into a jewelry store.

If you came up with *bring* and its beheadment, *ring*, you'd be right. Beheadments don't always rhyme, and sometimes one word is capitalized and the other is not, but the original word and its beheaded version will always fit into a sensible sentence. Some of the sentences will have multiple beheadments, where the first letter is chopped off more than once. Your brain challenge is to fill in each sentence with the original word followed by its beheadment(s). Now off with their heads!

TIMED PLAY:
To create a baseline of your processing speed for this puzzle type, time how long it takes you to complete the *first set* of exercises (Set One). Then time yourself again on the completion of the *last set* of exercises (Set Seven). Compare your two times. If your final time beats your original time, you've improved your processing speed for this type of mental stretch. Congratulations!

SET ONE:
NATURAL KINGDOM

1. You never know exactly _____ the _____ will lay its next egg.

2. His horse almost tripped on a _____ when he went riding on a dude _____.

3. It was so quiet; you could _____ a sheep and _____ the pieces of wool fall from behind its _____.

4. A _____ is an insect and an _____ is a snake.

5. A _____ mouse can be trained to pull a _____ and get a food pellet.

ANSWER KEY

BEHEADMENTS

Set One: Natural Kingdom

1. when, hen
2. branch, ranch
3. shear, hear, ear
4. wasp, asp
5. clever, lever

HOW TO PLAY:
See instructions on page 15.

SET TWO:
EDIBLES

1. Before my mom buys a loaf of _____, she'll _____ the label.

2. The seafaring _____ was _____ at the slow _____ at which his son _____ his food.

3. The _____ for a pound of _____ is more than that of _____.

4. The chocolate _____ she bought at the skating _____ is as dark as India _____.

5. _____ dessert item on the menu looks _____ good to me.

6. The aluminum _____ was dripping with olive _____.

7. Get the leftover _____ cereal out of the refrigerator, _____ it up in the microwave, then _____ it.

8. A small _____ should be _____ in helping you decide if you like a new ice-cream flavor.

9. You'll need four or five dollars for a burger and a _____ drink at the food court in the _____.

10. I put on my _____ and picked up some _____ cereal _____ the market.

ANSWER KEY

BEHEADMENTS

Set Two: Edibles

1. bread, read
2. pirate, irate, rate, ate
3. price, rice, ice
4. drink, rink, ink
5. Every, very
6. foil, oil
7. wheat, heat, eat
8. sample, ample
9. small, mall
10. coat, oat, at

BEHEADMENTS

HOW TO PLAY:
See instructions on page 15.

SET THREE:
SPORTS

1. It would be _____ to go _____ skating with you.

2. It will _____ you down when you put your bike into
   a _____ gear.

3. The skateboarder tried to do a fancy _____, but fell and
   cut his _____.

4. Sir Edmund Hillary didn't _____ until he got to the _____ of
   Mt. Everest.

5. I just _____ my head as I watched the bowling ball _____ into
   the gutter.

6. It was a moment of great _____ when Michael Jordan saw a
   replay of his winning jump shot in slow _____.

7. A good _____ for a basketball player is six foot _____.

ANSWER KEY

BEHEADMENTS

Set Three: Sports

1. nice, ice
2. slow, low
3. flip, lip
4. stop, top
5. shook, hook
6. emotion, motion
7. height, eight

BEHEADMENTS

HOW TO PLAY:
See instructions on page 15.

SET FOUR:
SMARTY PANTS

1. I can get a lot of information _____ an encyclopedia on a CD- _____.

2. You'll be worthy of much _____ if you can _____ that B to an A.

3. If anyone can _____ more _____ into this computer, I _____ going to be very surprised.

4. My older sister promised she'd _____ me _____ to use an Excel spreadsheet.

5. My cousin showed me how to play an F _____ on his _____.

6. Russia beat the United States into _____ because its science program moved along at a faster _____.

7. I learned about possessive pronouns like _____ and _____.

8. If you practice what you _____, you can _____ _____ and every one of your goals.

9. My parents call our home the most valuable piece of real _____ in the _____.

ANSWER KEY

BEHEADMENTS

Set Four: Smarty Pants

1. from, ROM
2. praise, raise
3. cram, RAM, am
4. show, how
5. sharp, harp
6. space, pace
7. your, our
8. preach, reach, each
9. estate, state

How to Play:
See instructions on page 15.

Set Five:
Says Who

1. Uncle Joe got a _____ on his foot from all the picketing he did when his _____ went out on strike.

2. Some people think a lucky _____ can keep them away from _____.

3. The wet rug may be _____ that there's a hole in the _____.

4. The _____ tried to _____ people into paying money for phony prizes.

5. It would be very strange to _____ a sneaker _____ on top of an _____ of clubs.

ANSWER KEY

BEHEADMENTS

Set Five: Says Who

1. bunion, union
2. charm, harm
3. proof, roof
4. crook, rook
5. place, lace, ace

BEHEADMENTS

HOW TO PLAY:
See instructions on page 15.

SET SIX:
I SUPPOSE

1. I think my parents will buy me that Halloween _____ if I _____ for it.

2. I suppose you can _____ the author if this puzzle is too _____.

3. Some people come _____ as being very _____.

4. A wooden _____ is one way to _____ down a vampire.

5. When my _____ does yoga, she chants, "_____."

ANSWER KEY

BEHEADMENTS

Set Six: I Suppose

1. mask, ask
2. blame, lame
3. across, cross
4. stake, take
5. mom, Om

BEHEADMENTS

HOW TO PLAY:
See instructions on page 15.

SET SEVEN:
OUTDOORS

1. The river may _____ up if another _____ falls into it.

2. It's not supposed to _____ anymore _____ that spring is here.

3. A drunk _____ drove right into the _____.

4. People go to the beach to play in the _____ _____ the water.

5. The farmer had to _____ the field even though the temperature was uncomfortably _____.

ANSWER KEY

BEHEADMENTS

Set Seven: Outdoors

1. clog, log
2. snow, now
3. driver, river
4. sand, and
5. plow, low

HOW TO PLAY:

Curtailments are like beheadments, except you chop away the last letter instead of the first one. Both beheadments and curtailments change words into *new* words with *new* meanings. Can you figure out the missing words in the curtailment below?

If the old man uses his _____, he _____ walk.

If you came up with *cane* and *can*, you'd be right. As with beheadments, the idea of the game is to place the original word and its curtailed version into a sentence. The original (longer) word is the first missing word in the sentence. Some sentences have multiple curtailments, where the last letter is chopped off more than once. However, it must always be a last letter and not one that comes before. (For instance, *bow* is not a curtailment of *blown*.) Now off with their tails!

TIMED PLAY:

To create a baseline of your processing speed for this puzzle type, time how long it takes you to complete Set One. Then time yourself again on the completion of Set Seven. Compare your two times. If your final time beats your original time, you've improved your processing speed for this type of mental stretch. Good job!

SET ONE:
FOOD STUFF

1. The way to find out how to make _____ of salmon is to look in the recipe _____.

2. Mom bought her silverware, china, and fine _____ in a store on the other side of the state _____.

3. I had a cheese enchilada with _____ beans and a _____ of milk.

4. The first three things I put into the shopping cart were a _____ onion, an Anjou _____, and a can of _____ soup.

5. Just as the batter squared around to _____, my hot dog fell out of the _____.

6. A _____ can't eat too much pie à la _____.

ANSWER KEY

CURTAILMENTS

Set One: Food Stuff

1. filet, file
2. linen, line
3. pinto, pint
4. pearl, pear, pea
5. bunt, bun
6. model, mode

CURTAILMENTS

HOW TO PLAY:
See instructions on page 29.

SET TWO:
MIXED BAG

1. It gave me a _____ to think I might have a _____ on my face.

2. I want to show _____ all that _____ best puzzle solver in the house is me.

3. Some people would rather _____ than shoot a _____ and arrow.

4. Cleaning all the _____ off the oven can be a pretty _____ task.

5. The _____ prince had some exotic pets, like a falcon and a _____.

6. A man with a _____ of Beethoven was waiting at the _____ stop.

7. I've been trying to fill out this order _____ _____ three days.

ANSWER KEY

CURTAILMENTS

Set Two: Mixed Bag

1. scare, scar
2. them, the
3. bowl, bow
4. grime, grim
5. crown, crow
6. bust, bus
7. form, for

CURTAILMENTS

HOW TO PLAY:
See instructions on page 29.

SET THREE:
UPS & DOWNS

1. The actress got her _____ five years ago then she went on to become a _____.

2. I'd be doing more puzzles now, but I've _____ to _____ to school.

3. When I was told I'd have to go on a _____, I thought I would _____.

4. After my uncle got a back _____, he spent a lot of time going to health _____.

5. Some people would rather sit down and _____ all day rather than _____ up the floor.

6. This is a _____ with high notes that his _____ sings _____ well.

7. I _____ the next dance is a bunny _____.

ANSWER KEY

CURTAILMENTS

Set Three: Ups & Downs

1. start, star
2. got, go
3. diet, die
4. spasm, spas
5. mope, mop
6. song, son, so
7. hope, hop

CURTAILMENTS

HOW TO PLAY:
See instructions on page 29.

SET FOUR:
COMMON SENSE

1. The telephone _____ and I _____ to answer it.

2. The _____ was _____ heavy to use, so I chose a lighter one.

3. If you _____ too much, it's time to get a _____ on yourself.

4. It's not a good _____ to be extremely fat or _____.

5. Every _____ has a _____-truck service you can go _____ if your car breaks down.

ANSWER KEY

CURTAILMENTS

Set Four: Common Sense

1. rang, ran
2. tool, too
3. gripe, grip
4. thing, thin
5. town, tow, to

CURTAILMENTS

HOW TO PLAY:
See instructions on page 29.

SET FIVE:
HEALTH CONCERNS

1. I don't think a _____ bite will cause you to have a
   nervous _____.

2. It's _____ to wash the _____ off your hands before you _____
   to the dinner table to eat.

3. Put a damp _____ on the wound until the blood begins
   to _____.

4. After I broke my _____, I couldn't _____ my saxophone _____ well.

5. My brother says that the best way to get through the daily _____
   is to _____ and bear it.

ANSWER KEY

CURTAILMENTS

Set Five: Health Concerns

1. tick, tic
2. good, goo, go
3. cloth, clot
4. tooth, toot, too
5. grind, grin

HOW TO PLAY:
See instructions on page 29.

SET SIX:
OUT & ABOUT

1. Most of the time, a _____ is _____ from the nearest big city.

2. If the rain doesn't _____ off, you may use your cassette-_____ player, but please _____ me on the shoulder if I fall asleep.

3. At the miniature-golf _____, _____ of our group made _____.

4. If I ever travel around the _____ in a _____, I'll _____ to bring something to read.

5. _____ year, I wonder if I will _____ go to Times Square on New Year's _____.

6. I spent a weekend in _____ Springs with a good _____ and his _____.

7. The _____ thought that a Cinco de _____ fiesta _____ be a good idea.

ANSWER KEY

CURTAILMENTS

Set Six: Out & About

1. farm, far
2. taper, tape, tap
3. party, part, par
4. planet, plane, plan
5. Every, ever, Eve
6. Palm, pal, pa
7. mayor, Mayo, may

HOW TO PLAY:
See instructions on page 29.

SET SEVEN:
MOVING OBJECTS

1. The car started to _____ on some ice during our _____ trip.

2. I told the _____ to heel, but he didn't _____ it.

3. You can't sail on this _____ with a _____ constrictor around your neck.

4. The _____ just kept jumping to and _____.

5. My favorite Saturday activities are to _____ down the highway and spend a day at the _____.

6. I tried to _____ through the water with a _____ of gum in my mouth.

ANSWER KEY

CURTAILMENTS

Set Seven: Moving Objects

1. skid, ski
2. dog, do
3. boat, boa
4. frog, fro
5. zoom, zoo
6. wade, wad

HOW TO PLAY:

A "palindrome" is a word, phrase, verse, or sentence that reads the same backward or forward. The word *dad* is an example of a simple, three-letter palindrome. In this game, you will be given a sentence with a missing word. The missing word is a palindrome. You will also be given a clue. The clue tells you the number of letters in the palindrome. Your challenge is to find the palindrome that will complete the sentence so it makes sense.

TIMED PLAY:

To create a baseline of your processing speed for this puzzle type, time how long it takes you to complete Palindrome 1. Then time yourself again on the completion of Palindrome 10. Compare your two times. If your final time beats your original time, you've improved your processing speed for this type of mental stretch. Well done!

1. Clue: 5 letters

   It is your _____ duty to vote.

2. Clue: 5 letters

   The boat was equipped with _____, which helped us determine direction and depth.

3. Clue: 6 letters

   As she became more embarrassed, the color of her face got _____.

4. Clue: 3 letters

   The anchored boat started to _____ on the water when the waves picked up.

5. Clue: 5 letters

   The teacher always told us to _____ to the dictionary if we weren't sure how to spell a word.

ANSWER KEY

PALINDROMES

1. civic
2. radar
3. redder
4. bob
5. refer

HOW TO PLAY:
See instructions on page 43.

6. Clue: 7 letters

   The wallpaper was old and peeling, so she decided to _____
   all the walls in her house.

7. Clue: 5 letters

   To ensure the picture was hanging evenly, she used a special
   tool called a _____.

8. Clue: 7 letters

   Unless you are an expert driver, you should never drive

   a _____ _____ on a speed track.

9. Clue: 7 letters

   He had a shoulder tear in his _____ cuff.

10. Clue: 5 letters

    Due to her excellent voice, she was given many _____
    in the school choir.

ANSWER KEY

PALINDROMES

6. repaper
7. level
8. race car
9. rotator
10. solos

HOW TO PLAY:

The idea in this game is to find a letter that can be put in front of each of the four given words, so that four new words can be formed with the same starting letter. For example, suppose that the four given words are: LIMB, HAIR, RASH, ORAL. If you put a "C" in front of each, you would get these four new words: CLIMB, CHAIR, CRASH, CORAL. In this exercise, find the common letter that can precede each given word set to form a whole new set of words.

TIMED PLAY:

To create a baseline of your processing speed for this puzzle type, time how long it takes you to complete Word Stretch, numbers 1–5. Then time yourself again on the completion of Word Stretch, numbers 6–10. Compare your two times. If your final time beats your original time, you've improved your processing speed for this type of mental stretch. High five!

Old Words	New Words
1. LANE, INCH, EACH, ROVE	
2. RAFT, READ, RIVER, EARTH	
3. RAIL, LASH, ETCH, LAME	
4. ROTE, OMEN, HACK, ITCH	
5. TORE, HARE, PORE, CARE	
6. AIL, ARM, EAR, ATE	
7. OFTEN, AILS, ADDLE, AGES	
8. WINE, ABLE, RACK, HERE	
9. WING, TART, LATE, WISH	
10. LEAN, OATS, ROCK, EASE	

ANSWER KEY

WORD STRETCH

1. plane, pinch, peach, prove
2. draft, dread, driver, dearth
3. frail, flash, fetch, flame
4. wrote, women, whack, witch
5. store, share, spore, scare
6. fail, farm, fear, fate
7. soften, sails, saddle, sages
8. twine, table, track, there
9. swing, start, slate, swish
10. clean, coats, crock, cease

HOW TO PLAY:

We read English words left to right. We know where the first letter is and in which direction the letters flow to form a word. Circular words pose a greater brain challenge because the first letter can be anywhere in the circle, and the word might be read clockwise or counterclockwise.

TIMED PLAY:

To create a baseline of your processing speed for this puzzle type, time how long it takes you to complete Set One. Then time yourself again on the completion of Set Five. Compare your two times. If your final time beats your original time, you've improved your processing speed for this type of mental stretch. Super!

SET ONE:

GIRLS' NAMES

```
        N                           F
   O         I              I           R
   R         C              N           E
   E         A              I           D
        V                       W


        R                       L
   O         R              Y           T
   L         A              N           I
   E         I              N           A
        N                       K
```

ANSWER KEY

CIRCULAR WORDS

Set One: Girls' Names

1. Veronica
2. Winifred
3. Lorraine
4. Kaitlynn

HOW TO PLAY:
See instructions on page 49.

SET TWO:
COUNTRIES

```
        G                           D
   U         A                 I         O
   T         L                 A         B
   R         P                 C         M
        O                           A


        G                           L
   L         A                 I         A
   U         R                 A         N
   B         I                 H         D
        A                           T
```

ANSWER KEY

CIRCULAR WORDS

Set Two: Countries

1. Portugal
2. Cambodia
3. Bulgaria
4. Thailand

How to Play:
See instructions on page 49.

Set Three:
Medical Words

```
        A                                    R

B               I                  B                 A

A               R                  E                 L

C               E                  R                 C

        T                                    E


        E                                    O

X               L                  T                 M

I               S                  P                 S

A               Y                  M                 S

        D                                    Y
```

ANSWER KEY

CIRCULAR WORDS

Set Three: Medical Words

1. bacteria
2. cerebral
3. dyslexia
4. symptoms

CIRCULAR WORDS

HOW TO PLAY:
See instructions on page 49.

SET FOUR:
WORDS WITH Qs

```
        W                                Q
A               K                I               U
U               S                N               E
        Q                                U



        L                                E
  I             C                  R             V
Q               E                Q               I
        U                                U
```

ANSWER KEY

CIRCULAR WORDS

Set Four: Words with Qs

1. squawk
2. unique
3. clique
4. quiver

HOW TO PLAY:
See instructions on page 49.

SET FIVE:
DOUBLE-LETTER WORDS

```
        D                                       S
  E           O                           A           S
  R           C                           P           T
  R           C                           S           R
        U                                       E


        E                                       Z
  T           R                           I           Z
  T           Y                           L           A
  A           F                           B           R
        L                                       D
```

ANSWER KEY

CIRCULAR WORDS

Set Five: Double-Letter Words

1. occurred
2. trespass
3. flattery
4. blizzard

Embedded Words

How to Play:

Many words share letters in common. Sometimes these shared letters form another word . . . a word within a word. For example, the words *scared* and *carpet* each share the letters *c*, *a*, *r*, and *e*, which form the embedded word *care*. In this game, you will be presented with a series of embedded words broken out by theme. For all five sets, your goal is to use the clue (in italics) to solve each word. This is not a timed puzzle.

Example: __ C A R E __: *frightened*

Please note: To increase flexibility, the answers that contain the embedded words do not relate at all to each set's theme!

Set One:
Coffee

A. Your embedded word is CUP:
  1. C __ UP __: *two-door car*
  2. C __ __ __ UP: *a Heinz product*
  3. C __ U __ P __ __: *to wrinkle*
  4. C U __ P __ __ __ __: *deserving blame*
  5. __ C U __ P __ __ __ __: *an art form*

B. Your embedded word is SIP:
  1. S I __ P __ __: *very easy*
  2. S __ __ I __ P: *a shellfish*
  3. S __ I P __ __ __: *a sum of money*
  4. __ __ __ __ S __ I P: *a European herb*
  5. S __ I __ __ __ P: *a horse rider's foot support*

C. Your embedded word is LID:
  1. __ L __ I D: *of a Scottish pattern*
  2. L I __ __ __ D: *noted as an item*
  3. L I __ __ __ __ D: *an oil used in paint*
  4. __ __ __ L __ I __ __ D: *took advantage of*
  5. __ __ L I __ __ __ __ D: *infinite*

ANSWER KEY

EMBEDDED WORDS

Set One: Coffee

A.

1. coupe
2. catsup
3. crumple
4. culpable
5. sculpture

B.

1. simple
2. shrimp
3. stipend
4. parsnip
5. stirrup

C.

1. plaid
2. listed
3. linseed
4. exploited
5. unlimited

EMBEDDED WORDS

HOW TO PLAY:
See instructions on page 59. *Please note*: To increase flexibility, the answers that contain the embedded words do not relate at all to each set's theme!

SET TWO:
OFFICE SUPPLIES

A. Your embedded word is PEN:
1. P __ E N __ __: *in abundance*
2. P E __ __ __ N __ __ T: *not subject to change*
3. __ __ __ P E N __: *a certain reptile*
4. P E N __ __ __ __: *part of a grandfather clock*
5. __ __ P E __ __ N __: *getting gradually smaller*

B. Your embedded word is INK:
1. __ __ I N K: *use the noggin*
2. __ __ __ I N K: *diminish*
3. I N K __ __ __ __: *suspicion*
4. I N __ __ K __: *consumption*
5. __ __ I N __ __ __ K __ __ __: *extremely detailed*

C. Your embedded word is UPS:
1. __ __ U P S: *minestrone and gazpacho, for example*
2. __ U __ P S: *sometimes they have to be taken*
3. __ __ U __ P __ __ S: *heralding instruments*
4. __ __ UP __ S: *what a temper sometimes does*
5. __ U P __ __ S __ __ __ __: *extremely fast*

ANSWER KEY

EMBEDDED WORDS

Set Two: Office Supplies

A.

1. plenty

2. permanent

3. serpent

4. pendulum

5. tapering

B.

1. think

2. shrink

3. inkling

4. intake

5. painstaking

C.

1. soups

2. lumps

3. trumpets

4. erupts

5. supersonic

HOW TO PLAY:

See instructions on page 59. *Please note*: To increase flexibility, the answers that contain the embedded words do not relate at all to each set's theme!

SET THREE:
SUPERMARKET

A. Your embedded word is MEAT:

1. M E A __ __ __ T: *most cruel*
2. __ __ M __ E __ A T __: *not too hot or cold*
3. __ M __ E __ __ __ __ A T __: *assume another identify*
4. __ __ M __ E __ __ A T __: *pay*
5. M E __ __ A __ __ T __: *untruthfulness*

B. Your embedded word is CAN:

1. C __ A __ N: *something with links*
2. C __ A N __ __ __ : *part of a skull*
3. __ __ __ C A N: *a bird found in South America, Mexico, and the Caribbean*
4. __ C __ A __ __ __ N: *a happening*
5. __ __ C __ A N __ __ __: *having mystical powers*

C. Your embedded word is RICE:

1. R I C __ E __ __: *superlative in net worth*
2. __ R I C __ __ __ E __: *more thorny*
3. __ R I C __ E __: *an insect*
4. R __ __ __ __ I C __ E __: *confined*
5. __ R I C __ __ __ __ E __: *mason*

ANSWER KEY

EMBEDDED WORDS

Set Three: Supermarket

A.

1. meanest
2. temperate
3. impersonate
4. compensate
5. mendacity

B.

1. chain
2. cranium
3. toucan
4. occasion
5. enchanted

C.

1. richest
2. pricklier
3. cricket
4. restricted
5. bricklayer

EMBEDDED WORDS

HOW TO PLAY:

See instructions on page 59. *Please note*: To increase flexibility, the answers that contain the embedded words do not relate at all to each set's theme!

SET FOUR:
FAMILY RESTAURANT

A. Your embedded word is EAT:

1. E A __ T __: *something that may quake*
2. __ E __ A T __ __ __ : *significant association*
3. __ E __ A __ T: *take back a statement*
4. __ __ E A T __ __ __ __: *medical care*
5. __ E __ __ __ __ A __ T: *plaintiff's adversary*

B. Your embedded word is PIE:

1. P __ I __ E: *a group of lions*
2. __ __ P I __ E: *a multinational political power*
3. __ __ __ P I __ E: *put together*
4. __ __ P __ I E __: *gave an answer*
5. __ __ __ P __ __ __ I __ E: *to settle differences*

C. Your embedded word is BLT (bacon, lettuce, tomato):

1. B __ __ L T: *constructed*
2. B __ L __ __ T: *exemplified by* Swan Lake
3. B __ L __ __ T __ __: *a short publication*
4. B L __ __ T __ __: *possible result of too much sun*
5. __ __ B L __ __ __ __ T __: *a certain furniture covering*

ANSWER KEY

EMBEDDED WORDS

Set Four: Family Restaurant

A.

1. earth
2. relation
3. recant
4. treatment
5. defendant

B.

1. pride
2. empire
3. compile
4. replied
5. compromise

C.

1. built
2. ballet
3. bulletin
4. blister
5. tablecloth

EMBEDDED WORDS

How to Play:

See instructions on page 59. *Please note*: To increase flexibility, the answers that contain the embedded words do not relate at all to each set's theme!

Set Five:
Medical Office

A. Your embedded word is DOC:

1. D O C _ _ _: *a museum tour guide*
2. D O _ _ _ _ _ C: *home related*
3. _ D O _ _ _ C _ _ _: *teenage*
4. D _ _ _ O _ _ C: *acting as a tyrant*
5. D _ _ O _ _ _ _ _ C: *in a fair manner*

B. Your embedded word is LVN (Licensed Vocational Nurse):

1. L _ V _ N: *to make fresher*
2. _ _ L V _ N _: *dividing by two*
3. _ _ L _ _ V _ N _: *having faith*
4. _ _ L V _ _ _ _ N: *a religious goal*
5. _ _ L V _ N: *woodsy*

C. Your embedded word is CARE:

1. C A R _ E _: *rug*
2. _ C A R E _: *frightened*
3. C _ A R _ _ _ E _: *a person in a play*
4. C _ A R _ _ E _: *a woodwind*
5. _ C A R _ E _: *Pimpernel*

ANSWER KEY

EMBEDDED WORDS

Set Five: Medical Office

A.

1. docent

2. domestic

3. adolescent

4. despotic

5. democratic

B.

1. liven

2. halving

3. believing

4. salvation

5. sylvan

C.

1. carpet

2. scared

3. character

4. clarinet

5. Scarlet

WORD MULTIPLIER

HOW TO PLAY:

You will be presented with four sets of grids, each containing letters that make up a common word. Your challenge is to mix and match the letters to make as many new words as possible. Each new word should contain four or more letters. Vowels can be used more than once in the same new word. You will be playing against a computer program that generated new words, based on the letters in each grid. How many new words can you come up with? See if you can match or beat the computer!

SET ONE:

LATER GATOR

When presented with this challenge, the computer found 11 words with four letters or more.

L		A
	T	
E		R

NEW WORDS:

ANSWER KEY

WORD MULTIPLIER

Set One: Later Gator

alert, alter, earl, late, leer, rate, real, reel, tale, teal, tear

HOW TO PLAY:
See instructions on page 69.

SET TWO:
REACH FOR THE STARS

When presented with this challenge, the computer found 11 words with four letters.

R		E
	A	
H		C

NEW WORDS:

ANSWER KEY

WORD MULTIPLIER

Set Two: Reach for the Stars

ache, acre, arch, area, care, char, each, hare, hear, here, race

HOW TO PLAY:
See instructions on page 69.

SET THREE:
BRAWNY BRAINS

When presented with this challenge, the computer found at least 17 words with four letters or more.

B	A	N
R	I	S

NEW WORDS:

ANSWER KEY

WORD MULTIPLIER

Set Three: Brawny Brains

airs, aria(s), bars, barn(s), bans, basin, bias, bins, brain, bran, bras, bris, ibis, nabs, rain(s), ribs, sari

HOW TO PLAY:

See instructions on page 69.

SET FOUR:

TAKE A BREATH

When presented with this challenge, the computer found 36 words with four letters or more.

B	E	T
R	A	H

NEW WORDS:

ANSWER KEY

WORD MULTIPLIER

Set Four: Take a Breath

abate, area, bath, bathe, beater, beret, bare, bear, beat, beater, beer, beet, berate, berth, beta, brat, earth, eater, ether, hare, heart, hate, hater, hear, heat, heater, herb, here, rate, rebate, rehab, retreat, tear, there, three, tree

HOW TO PLAY:

This game is a recognition exercise. You are challenged to combine 20 divided words into 20 whole words by matching the front and back halves of each word. The words are not necessarily divided by syllable. For example, you might have "TRIU" and "MPH," which combined together would be "TRIUMPH." Cross off your matches as you go along. Also, some halves may not have a match.

TIMED PLAY:

To create a baseline of your processing speed for this puzzle type, time how long it takes you to complete Set One. Then time yourself again on the completion of Set Two. Compare your two times. If your final time beats your original time, you've improved your processing speed for this type of mental stretch. Wow!

SET ONE:
COMMON & EXOTIC PETS

OG	GER	CHI	TUR	HOG
KEET	RAB	MON	PARA	CRAB
FER	TLE	SN	CHIN	TARAN
HERMIT	HAM	LI	MA	WALLA
SE	HEDGE	KEY	BIL	AKE
PIR	BY	THON	RET	PY
ZARD	TULA	ANHA	CHILLA	CAW
STER	HOR	FR	HUAHUA	BIT

ANSWER KEY

WORD KNITTING

Set One: Common & Exotic Pets

frog, gerbil, hamster, hedgehog, parakeet, rabbit, hermit crab, Chihuahua, lizard, wallaby, python, monkey, piranha, tarantula, turtle, ferret, horse, snake, macaw, chinchilla

HOW TO PLAY:
See instructions on page 77.

SET TWO:
SPICES

PER	SAF	BA	SPICE	ORE
OVE	ME	CIL	TARR	NUT
GANO	AGON	GE	ROSE	CUR
LIC	GER	GAR	PEP	CH
MEG	ANDER	PAP	CORI	CL
MON	SLEY	CINNA	PAR	SA
RIKA	ALL	GIN	FRON	RY
MARY	IVE	THY	SIL	ANTRO

ANSWER KEY

WORD KNITTING

Set Two: Spices

clove, oregano, tarragon, saffron, basil, nutmeg, curry, sage, coriander, garlic, rosemary, thyme, paprika, cinnamon, parsley, chive, cilantro, pepper, allspice, ginger

HOW TO PLAY:

A *ditloid* is a type of word puzzle in which a phrase, quotation, or fact must be deduced from the numbers and abbreviated letters in the clue. Common words such as 'the,' 'in,' 'a,' 'an,' 'of,' etc., are usually not abbreviated. Here is an example:

12 S of the Z = 12 signs of the Zodiac

In this logic challenge, you must use the numbers and letters as clues to decipher the common phrase or place(s). A clue is given for each Ditloid. First try to solve the Ditloids with the clues in the right column covered up with your hand or a piece of paper. If you get stuck, take a peek at the clue.

SET ONE

Ditloid	Clue
1. 101 D	Disney movie
2. 3 B M	nursery rhyme
3. The 10 C	biblical movie
4. 20,000 L U the S	Can you swim?
5. A B and the 40 T	Arabian tale

ANSWER KEY

DITLOID PUZZLES

Set One

1. *101 Dalmatians*
2. "Three Blind Mice"
3. *The Ten Commandments*
4. *20,000 Leagues Under the Sea*
5. "Ali Baba and the 40 Thieves"

HOW TO PLAY:
See instructions on page 81.

SET TWO

Ditloid	Clue
1. A the W in 80 D	travel-adventure bet
2. 2½ M	TV series
3. 7 B for 7 B	1950s musical
4. N 10 D S	famous address
5. The 7 W of the W	travel bucket list

ANSWER KEY

DITLOID PUZZLES

Set Two

1. *Around the World in 80 Days*

2. *Two and a Half Men*

3. *Seven Brides for Seven Brothers*

4. Number 10 Downing Street

5. The Seven Wonders of the World

HOW TO PLAY:

Your brain challenge is to discover the word that can be added to a quadruplet set of words to form new words or phrases. The word they have in common may go before or after the presented word. The puzzle title is your clue to the word that can be glued to all four words. Or start with the set and work your way back to solving the puzzle title. When you decode the puzzle title, you will have the "common" word that completes the set.

Look at the example in the box below.

> ### TITLE: AN AMERICAN PASTIME
> 1. black
> 2. park
> 3. point
> 4. fire

What compound word does the title refer to? That's right, baseball. Now which half of this compound word can be linked to the four words in the set to create four new compound words? If you guessed ball, you're right again. Put it to the test: add ball to each of the words below (as a prefix or suffix) and see what you get. You've succeeded if your four new words are: *blackball*, *ballpark*, *ballpoint*, and *fireball*.

TIMED PLAY:

To create a baseline of your processing speed for this puzzle type, time how long it takes you to complete Sets 1–9. Then time yourself again on the completion of Sets 10–18. Compare your two times. If your final time beats your original time, you've improved your processing speed for this type of mental stretch. Congratulations!

SET ONE:

FORMER CATERPILLAR

1. dragon
2. fire
3. bar
4. swatter

ANSWER KEY

QUADRUPLETS

Set One: Former Caterpillar
fly—butterfly

QUADRUPLETS

HOW TO PLAY:
See instructions on page 85.

SET TWO:
ICY FIGURE

1. shoe
2. storm
3. board
4. flake

SET THREE:
BOATER'S SOS

1. birth
2. light
3. dream
4. dooms

ANSWER KEY

QUADRUPLETS

Set Two: Icy Figure
snow—snowman

Set Three: Boater's SOS
day—Mayday

QUADRUPLETS

HOW TO PLAY:
See instructions on page 85.

SET FOUR:
MAD DRIVER

1. rail
2. runner
3. show
4. race

SET FIVE:
PRISON INMATE

1. cage
2. humming
3. brain
4. blue

ANSWER KEY

QUADRUPLETS

Set Four: Mad Driver
road—road rage

Set Five: Prison Inmate
bird—jailbird

QUADRUPLETS

HOW TO PLAY:
See instructions on page 85.

SET SIX:
DEODORANT PLACE

1. rest
2. fire
3. fore
4. chair

SET SEVEN:
DENTIST'S FRIEND

1. ache
2. pick
3. decay
4. fairy

ANSWER KEY

QUADRUPLETS

Set Six: Deodorant Place
arm—armpit

Set Seven: Dentist's Friend
tooth—toothbrush

QUADRUPLETS

HOW TO PLAY:
See instructions on page 85.

SET EIGHT:
OFFICE PEN

1. beach
2. game
3. park
4. goof

SET NINE:
SOAPY LIQUID

1. fall
2. balloon
3. color
4. melon

ANSWER KEY

QUADRUPLETS

Set Eight: Office Pen
ball—ballpoint

Set Nine: Soapy Liquid
water—dishwater

HOW TO PLAY:
See instructions on page 85.

SET TEN:
A LIE

1. knight
2. neighbor
3. adult
4. wink

SET ELEVEN:
MONEY WAD

1. book
2. data
3. robber
4. river

ANSWER KEY

QUADRUPLETS

Set Ten: A Lie
hood—falsehood

Set Eleven: Money Wad
bank—bankroll

QUADRUPLETS

HOW TO PLAY:
See instructions on page 85.

SET TWELVE:
TONE-DEAF SINGER

1. board
2. hole
3. latch
4. turn

SET THIRTEEN:
OLD-TIME MUSIC PLAYER

1. kick
2. mail
3. pill
4. boom

SET FOURTEEN:
SWEET-SMELLING FLOWER

1. comb
2. bunch
3. moon
4. dew

ANSWER KEY

QUADRUPLETS

Set Twelve: Tone-Deaf Singer
key—off key

Set Thirteen: Old-Time Music Player
box—jukebox

Set Fourteen: Sweet-Smelling Flower
honey—honeysuckle

QUADRUPLETS

HOW TO PLAY:
See instructions on page 85.

SET FIFTEEN:
GIRL'S COMMON HAIRDO
1. shirt
2. bone
3. gate
4. spin

SET SIXTEEN:
TICK OFF
1. post
2. bench
3. pock
4. down

SET SEVENTEEN:
HEAVEN BOUND

1. boat
2. saver
3. style
4. wild

SET EIGHTEEN
HUNTER'S WEAPON
1. tie
2. legged
3. rain
4. cross

ANSWER KEY

QUADRUPLETS

Set Fifteen: Girl's Common Hairdo
tail—ponytail

Set Sixteen: Tick Off
mark—checkmark

Set Seventeen: Heaven Bound
life—afterlife

Set Eighteen: Hunter's Weapon
bow—bow and arrow

PART 2:
RIGHT BRAIN

Can You See It?

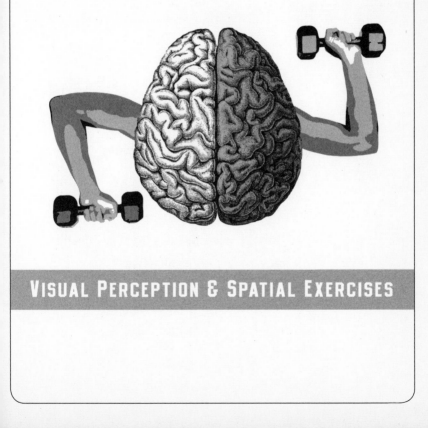

Visual Perception & Spatial Exercises

RIGHT BRAIN: CAN YOU SEE IT?
VISUAL PERCEPTION & SPATIAL EXERCISES

INTRODUCTION:

The focus of the exercises in this section will be on the right brain's visual-spatial processing strengths. In this workout, your brain will light up as it "sees" the possibilities in the patterns. The puzzles relate to:

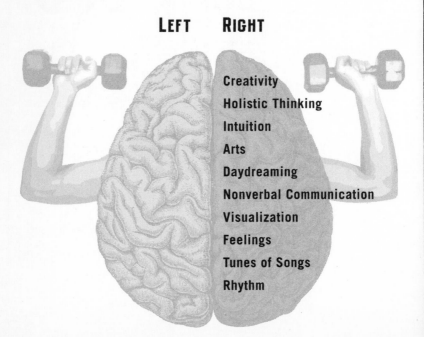

LEFT   RIGHT

Creativity

Holistic Thinking

Intuition

Arts

Daydreaming

Nonverbal Communication

Visualization

Feelings

Tunes of Songs

Rhythm

COMPARE AND CONTRAST

HOW TO PLAY:
In this exercise, you will see two pictures side by side that appear to be exact replicas. But they are not. Your challenge is to identify how the second picture is different from the first. It may have things missing, or things added to it. In each of the following three sets, there are five differences between the first image and the second image.

TIMED PLAY:
To create a baseline of your processing speed for this puzzle type, time how long it takes you to complete Set One. Then time yourself again on how long it takes you to complete Set Three. Compare your two times. If your final time beats your original time, you've improved your processing speed for this type of mental stretch. Congratulations!

SET ONE:
MERRY-GO-ROUND

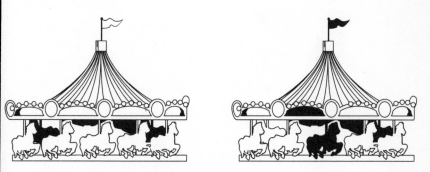

Find the five differences between the two images.

ANSWER KEY

COMPARE AND CONTRAST

Set One: Merry-Go-Round

1. The flag is filled in.

2. The second semicircular shape above the horses is filled in.

3. The third semicircular shape above the horses is missing a fifth bulb.

4. The horse in the center is filled in.

5. On the extreme left of the merry-go-round, the horse in back has changed from black to white.

 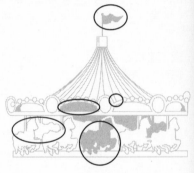

Compare and Contrast

How to Play:
See instructions on page 103.

Set Two:
Bird or Fish

Find the five differences between the two images.

ANSWER KEY

COMPARE AND CONTRAST

Set Two: Bird or Fish

1. The first head plume (moving from left to right) is missing a feather.

2. The third head plume (moving from left to right) is missing an additional shape.

3. The middle tail plume is missing a circular shape at the top.

4. Three small feathers are missing under the middle belly.

5. An inner shape is missing on the first leg.

HOW TO PLAY:
See instructions on page 103.

SET THREE:
HIEROGLYPHICS

Find the five differences between the two images.

ANSWER KEY

COMPARE AND CONTRAST

Set Three: Hieroglyphics

1. The small dot in the circle on the upper left is not filled in.

2. The interior line is missing from the curved shape on the upper left.

3. The first horizontal "leg" on the left is missing.

4. The small square shape at the bottom of the vertical "legs" has changed from white to black.

5. The bottom right-hand dot is missing.

HOW TO PLAY:

In this exercise, you will be presented with a set of images. All but one of the images appear in the mosaic picture that follows. Your brain challenge is to identify the image that is not part of the collage.

TIMED PLAY:

To create a baseline of your processing speed for this puzzle type, time how long it takes you to complete Set One. Then time yourself again on the completion of Set Four. Compare your two times. If your final time beats your original time, you've improved your processing speed for this type of mental stretch. Terrific!

SET ONE:
FLORAL

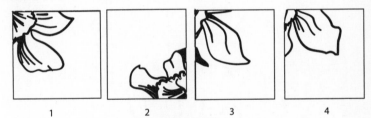

1 2 3 4

ANSWER KEY

MOSAICS

Set One: Floral

Image 3 is not part of the mosaic.

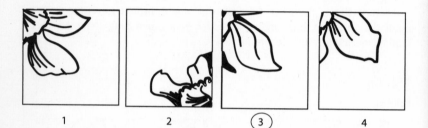

1   2   ③   4

HOW TO PLAY:
See instructions on page 109.

SET TWO:
HAWK

1   2   3   4

ANSWER KEY

MOSAICS

Set Two: Hawk

Image 1 is not part of the mosaic.

1

2

3

4

HOW TO PLAY:
See instructions on page 109.

SET THREE:
POT OF GOLD

1

2

3

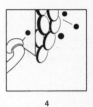

4

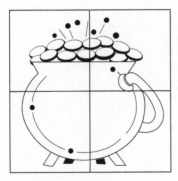

ANSWER KEY

MOSAICS

Set Three: Pot of Gold

Image 1 is not part of the mosaic.

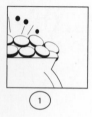

1

2

3

4

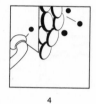

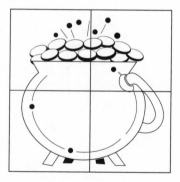

HOW TO PLAY:
See instructions on page 109.

SET FOUR:
DRAGONFLY

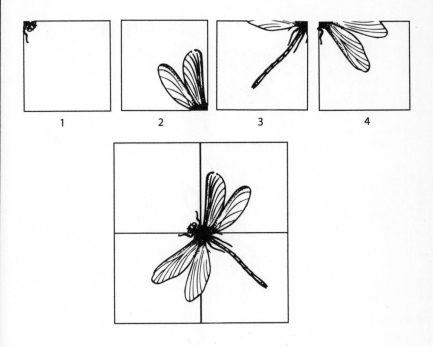

ANSWER KEY

MOSAICS

Set Four: Dragonfly

Image 2 is not part of the mosaic.

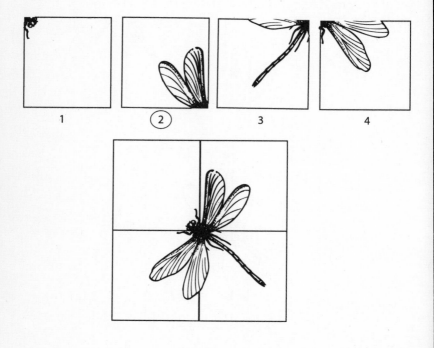

Entanglements

How to Play:

In this brain teaser, you will see a layered image. Your challenge is to identify and circle the three singular images that must be combined to create the layered image at the top.

TIMED PLAY:

To create a baseline of your processing speed for this puzzle type, time how long it takes you to complete Set One. Then time yourself again on the completion of Set Four. Compare your two times. If your final time beats your original time, you've improved your processing speed for this type of mental stretch. Well done!

Set One:
Foodie

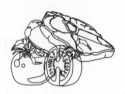

1

2

3

4

5

6

7

8

9

ANSWER KEY

ENTANGLEMENTS

Set One: Foodie

Images 3, 5, and 8 create the layered image at the top.

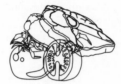

1

2

3

4

5

6

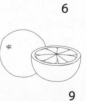

7

8

9

HOW TO PLAY:
See instructions on page 117.

SET TWO:
TOOLS

1

2

3

4

5

6

7

8

9

ANSWER KEY

ENTANGLEMENTS

Set Two: Tools

Images 2, 5, and 9 create the layered image at the top.

1

2

3

4

5

6

7

8

9

ENTANGLEMENTS

HOW TO PLAY:
See instructions on page 117.

SET THREE:
AEROBICS

1

2

3

4

5

6

7

8

9

ANSWER KEY

ENTANGLEMENTS

Set Three: Aerobics

Images 1, 5, and 9 create the layered image at the top.

HOW TO PLAY:
See instructions on page 117.

SET FOUR:
ZOO

ANSWER KEY

ENTANGLEMENTS

Set Four: Zoo

Images 6, 7, and 9 create the layered image at the top.

ODD ONE OUT

HOW TO PLAY:

In each of the following four sets, you will see a group of images. Try to find the image that is different from the rest. In the example below, can you guess which letter is the odd one out?

C B Q W D

All the letters in the example have curved lines, except for only one letter, which has straight lines. "W" is the odd one out.

TIMED PLAY:

To create a baseline of your processing speed for this puzzle type, time how long it takes you to complete Set One. Then time yourself again on the completion of Set Four. Compare your two times. If your final time beats your original time, you've improved your processing speed for this type of mental stretch. Bravo!

SET ONE:
CIRCLES & SHAPES

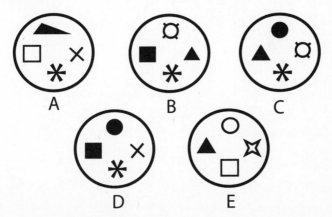

Which circle contains images that don't fit with the pattern of the others?

ANSWER KEY

ODD ONE OUT

Set One: Circles & Shapes

The answer is D. This is the only image that has all the shapes inside filled in. The other images have at least one shape that is not filled in.

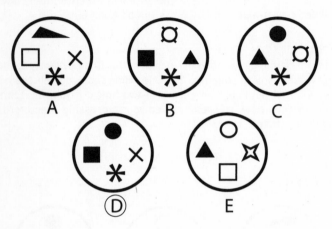

ODD ONE OUT

HOW TO PLAY:
See instructions on page 125.

SET TWO:
BOXES, DOTS & LINES

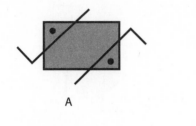

A

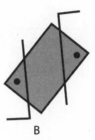

B

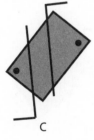

C

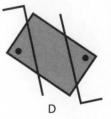

D

E

Which image doesn't fit the pattern?

ANSWER KEY

ODD ONE OUT

Set Two: Boxes, Dots & Lines

The answer is C. This is the only image in which the "L" lines don't create two triangles within the rectangle.

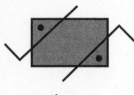

A

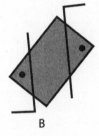

B

C

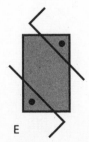

E

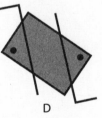

D

How to Play:
See instructions on page 125.

Set Three:
Olives & Toothpicks

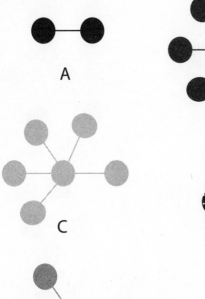

A

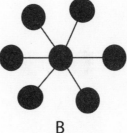

B

C

D

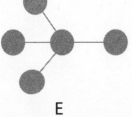

E

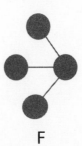

F

Which image doesn't fit the pattern?

ANSWER KEY

ODD ONE OUT

Set Three: Olives & Toothpicks

The answer is D. All of the other images are solid-color circles, but the circles in D have a dot pattern.

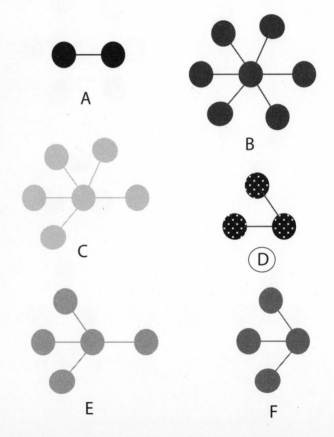

HOW TO PLAY:
See instructions on page 125.

SET FOUR:
POINTS

A

B

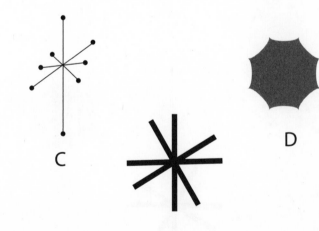

C

D

E

Which image doesn't fit the pattern?

ANSWER KEY

ODD ONE OUT

Set Four: Points

The answer is B. The other shapes have eight points, while the image in B has only seven points.

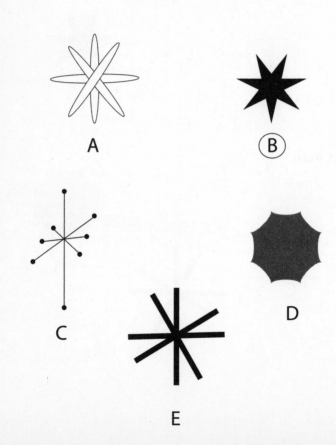

A

B

C

D

E

HOW TO PLAY:

In the next four sets, your brain challenge is to identify the object that would logically complete the sequence. The key to the sequence is in the visual pattern. Use your left brain to find the "rule" that orders the pattern, and your right brain to see the visual aspects of the pattern. Select the image that would come next in the sequence. Choose from shapes A, B, C, or D below for the answer.

TIMED PLAY:

To create a baseline of your processing speed for this puzzle type, time how long it takes you to complete Set One. Then time yourself again on the completion of Set Four. Compare your two times. If your final time beats your original time, you've improved your processing speed for this type of mental stretch. Good work!

SET ONE:
SPIN THE WHEEL

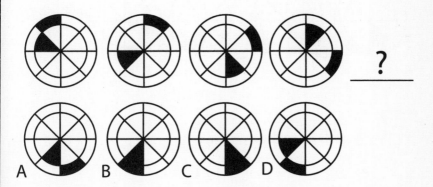

?

A   B   C   D

ANSWER KEY

NEXT IN LINE

Set One: Spin the Wheel

The answer is A. The correct answer takes the movement within both rings into account. The black rectangle section in the outer ring is moving clockwise one space. The black triangle section in the inner ring is moving counterclockwise one space.

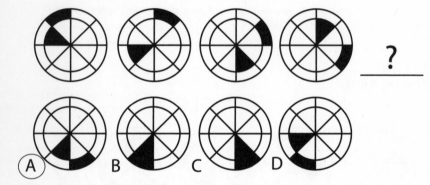

HOW TO PLAY:
See instructions on page 133.

SET TWO:
STAR PATTERN

ANSWER KEY

NEXT IN LINE

Set Two: Star Pattern

The answer is C. The two balls are following the broad path that is necessary to create the star if you were to do so without taking your pen off the paper. The next logical stop for the first ball is the bottom right tip. The second ball moves to the position the first ball just left.

HOW TO PLAY:
See instructions on page 133.

SET THREE:
CONNECT FOUR

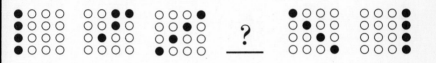

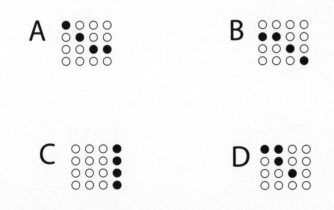

ANSWER KEY

NEXT IN LINE

Set Three: Connect Four

The answer is D, because each of the first three shapes has a mirror image in the next three shapes.

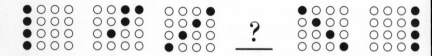

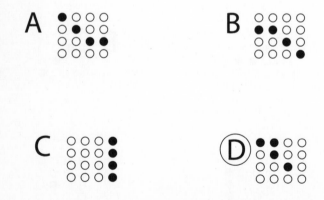

HOW TO PLAY:
See instructions on page 133.

SET FOUR:
SHAPE & DOT

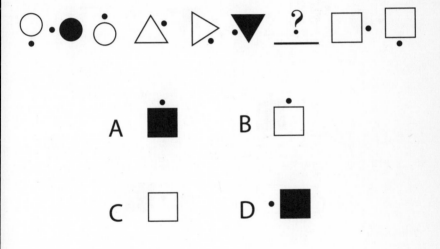

A

B

C

D

ANSWER KEY

NEXT IN LINE

Set Four: Shape & Dot

The answer is A. The sequence has three shapes: one that is solid, and two that are outlined. Each shape in the sequence has a dot on one side, which is being rotated one "click" in a clockwise direction.

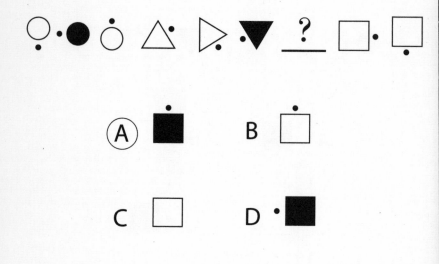

HOW TO PLAY:

This exercise involves both memory and visual perception. You have two grids: one has a graphic design superimposed on it, and the other one is blank. Your brain challenge is to reproduce the graphic design on the left by drawing every element of it in the same location on the blank grid on the right.

TIMED PLAY:

You have three minutes to create the reproduction. You may start anywhere in the design. Ready, set, go!

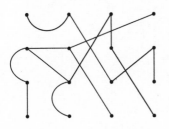 

ANSWER KEY

COPYCAT

Compare your graphic grid to the original grid. How close did you come to a perfect reproduction?

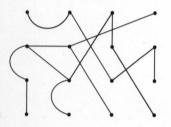 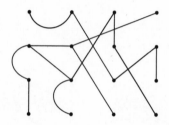

HOW TO PLAY:

In this brain challenge, you will be presented with two optical illusions. Optical illusions play tricks with the way your brain receives visual stimuli. For each illusion, a question will be posed. Answering the question will help you see your way toward solving the illusion.

SET ONE:
ARROWS & CATS

How many inside and outside arrows do you see in the figure below left?
How many cats do you see in the figure below right?

ANSWER KEY

OPTICAL ILLUSIONS

Set One: Arrows & Cats

Arrows = 8 [four black and four white]

Cats = 2 [one black and one white]

HOW TO PLAY:
See instructions on page 143.

SET TWO:
YOUNG WOMAN, OLD WOMAN

Can you see the young woman and the old woman in this same drawing?

ANSWER KEY

OPTICAL ILLUSIONS

Set Two: Young Woman, Old Woman

Young woman: The young woman is in a full profile — see her shapely chin and long neck with a choker?

Old woman: The young woman's chin becomes the nose of the old woman; the young woman's choker becomes the mouth of the old woman; the young woman's left ear becomes the left eye of the old woman.

PART 3: WHOLE BRAIN

CAN YOU THINK IT?

INTUITIVE-THINKING EXERCISES

WHOLE BRAIN: CAN YOU THINK IT?
INTUITIVE-THINKING EXERCISES

INTRODUCTION:
In this workout section, you will be called on to use whole-brain thinking, which involves both sides of the brain working somewhat simultaneously. Your left brain will apply logic, while your right brain will use a more visual and intuitive approach. Combining left- and right-brain thinking often leads to "out of the box" solutions.

LEFT

Logic
Analysis
Sequencing
Linear Reasoning
Mathematics
Language
Facts
Thinking in Words
Words of Songs
Computation

RIGHT

Creativity
Imagination
Holistic Thinking
Intuition
Arts
Rhythm
Nonverbal Communication
Visualization
Feelings
Tunes of Songs
Daydreaming

How to Play:

AHA! puzzles are those frustrating and challenging puzzles with answers that seem "obvious" — *after* you solve them. However, in order to get to the obvious answer, your brain needs to do some complex parallel processing that synthesizes input from both the left- and right-brain hemispheres. Solving AHA! puzzles requires creative thinking, and the answers often come in a flash of awareness. You cannot simply "think" the solutions to these puzzles in a traditional sense. Rather, you will need to draw on both logic and visual perception.

Set One:
Temperature Reading

Is this mug of coffee warm, lukewarm, or cool, and how do you know?

ANSWER KEY

AHA! PUZZLES

Set One: Temperature Reading

The coffee is cool. Mentally flip the image so that the fingers are on the top. The fingers holding the cup now spell out the word "cool."

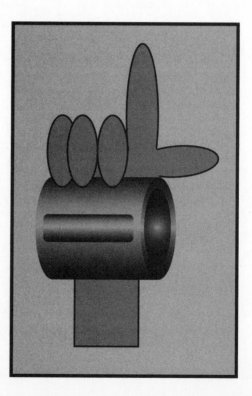

How to Play:

See instructions on page 149.

Set Two:
Cinderspeller

What animal's name has been used to create this demonic-looking cat with a forked tail?

ANSWER KEY

AHA! PUZZLES

Set Two: Cinderspeller

A mouse. The shapes (starting with the ears, then moving down and over to the tail) spell out M–O–U–S–E.

AHA! PUZZLES

HOW TO PLAY:
See instructions on page 149.

SET THREE:
SPOT-ON

Can you fill in the missing spot?

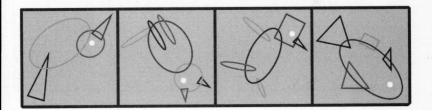

ANSWER KEY

AHA! PUZZLES

Set Three: Spot-On

Box 2 requires a second spot to complete the front view of the cat's two eyes.

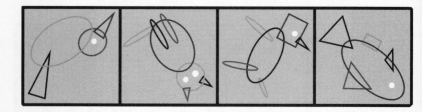

RHYME MAKER

HOW TO PLAY:
Each of the following phrases can be translated into a rhyming pair of words. For example the combination "pallid man" can become the rhyming pair "pale male."

SET ONE:
NATURAL KINGDOM

Phrases Rare	Rhyming Pair
1. Black Sea predator	
2. obese rodent	
3. comical hare	
4. swine toupee	

ANSWER KEY

RHYME MAKER

Set One: Natural Kingdom

1. dark shark
2. fat rat
3. funny bunny
4. pig wig

RHYME MAKER

HOW TO PLAY:
See instructions on page 155.

SET TWO:
SHIP AHOY

Phrases Rare	Rhyming Pair
1. big cargo boat	
2. crazy flat boat	
3. nap on a passenger ship	

ANSWER KEY

RHYME MAKER

Set Two: Ship Ahoy

1. large barge
2. daft raft
3. cruise snooze

HOW TO PLAY:
See instructions on page 155.

SET THREE:
FOOD FEAST

Phrases Rare	Rhyming Pair
1. goody for carnivores	
2. meal for ocean life	
3. washed legume	

ANSWER KEY

RHYME MAKER

Set Three: Food Feast

1. meat treat
2. fish dish
3. clean bean

How to Play:

A "rebus" is a pictorial representation of a name, word, or common phrase. To solve the following eight sets of rebus riddles, you must combine your visual and verbal perceptions to lead you to a creative answer. The example below illustrates how the thought process works. In this example, the word "head" is placed over the word "heels." The black line represents the over/under relationship. Put the visual and verbal clues together, and you get the common expression "head over heels."

HEAD
_____ = *HEAD OVER HEELS*
HEELS

TIMED PLAY:

To create a baseline of your processing speed for this puzzle type, time how long it takes you to complete Sets 1–4. Then time yourself again on the completion of Sets 5–8. Compare your two times. If your final time beats your original time, you've improved your processing speed for this type of mental stretch. Congratulations!

Set One:
Crowd Control

10   **1**   **2**

9   **3**

8   **SAFETY**   **4**

7   **5**

6

ANSWER KEY

REBUS RIDDLES

Set One: Crowd Control

safety in numbers

HOW TO PLAY:
See instructions on page 161.

SET TWO:
NOT MAKING ANY HEADWAY

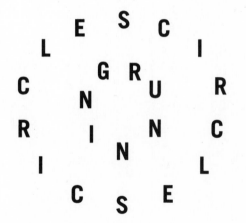

ANSWER KEY

REBUS RIDDLES

Set Two: Not Making Any Headway
running in circles

How to Play:
See instructions on page 161.

Set Three:
LOL

1. Funny

2. Funny

1. Word

2. Word

3. Word

4. Word

ANSWER KEY

REBUS RIDDLES

Set Three: LOL
too funny for words

HOW TO PLAY:
See instructions on page 161.

SET FOUR:
PROTEIN BREAKFAST

E	G	S	G		G	E	S	G
S	E	G	G		S	G	E	G
S	G	E	G		G	G	S	E

ANSWER KEY

REBUS RIDDLES

Set Four: Protein Breakfast

scrambled eggs

HOW TO PLAY:
See instructions on page 161.

SET FIVE:
LET'S FIGHT

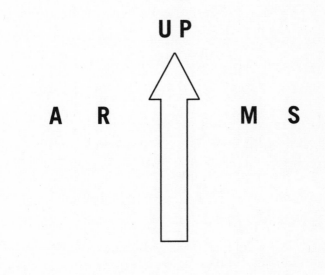

ANSWER KEY

REBUS RIDDLES

Set Five: Let's Fight

up in arms

How to Play:
See instructions on page 161.

Set Six:
So Sorry

Give	**Get**
Give	**Get**
+	
Give	**Get**
Give	**Get**

ANSWER KEY

REBUS RIDDLES

Set Six: So Sorry
forgive and forget

How to Play:
See instructions on page 161.

Set Seven:
Pushing Daisies

G R O U N D

FEET   **FEET**

FEET   **FEET**

FEET   **FEET**

ANSWER KEY

REBUS RIDDLES

Set Seven: Pushing Daisies

six feet underground

HOW TO PLAY:
See instructions on page 161.

SET EIGHT:
BREAK UP

ANSWER KEY

REBUS RIDDLES

Set Eight: Break Up

misunderstanding between friends

HOW TO PLAY:

Each of the four riddles that follow contains a concealed truth. Solve the riddle and find the truth. Riddles are not difficult to solve if you use your imagination and trust your intuition. Often the truths hidden in riddles are quite simple and just require a little "out of the box" thinking.

TIMED PLAY:

To create a baseline of your processing speed for this puzzle type, time how long it takes you to complete Set One. Then time yourself again on the completion of Set Four. Compare your two times. If your final time beats your original time, you've improved your processing speed for this type of mental stretch. Top-notch!

SET ONE:

AT THE BALLET

Brian is eating his favorite health-food snack. In order to eat it, he needs a special tool. When he thinks of this tool, he often thinks of his favorite ballet. What is the name of the tool?

SET TWO:

AT THE RESTAURANT

Gracie is in a fine restaurant. Everyone around her is eating and drinking. Gracie is carrying a glass of wine in her hand. Although she enjoys a glass of wine from time to time, she will not take one sip tonight. What is Gracie doing?

ANSWER KEY

MINI MYSTERIES

Set One: At the Ballet
nutcracker

Set Two: At the Restaurant
cocktail waitressing

HOW TO PLAY:
See instructions on page 177.

SET THREE:
AT HOME
Lucy owns a house, but she only uses it during the winter-holiday season. While she admires it from the outside, she never steps inside. At the end of the season the house is gone, only to be rebuilt again next year. She is not a carpenter. Her houses always have a wonderful smell, but she doesn't use air fresheners. What kind of a house is it?

SET FOUR:
AT AN EVENT
Julia puts on a disguise and heads out for the evening. She goes to a building filled with people and seats. Everyone is facing a large screen. She sits there for about 2 hours, during which she sees her own image many times over on the screen. Afterwards, she sneaks out so she will not be recognized by the crowd. Who is Julia?

ANSWER KEY

MINI MYSTERIES

Set Three: At Home
gingerbread house

Set Four: At an Event
an actress in the film

FILL IN THE PUN

HOW TO PLAY:

A *pun* is a form of wordplay that suggests two or more meanings, by exploiting multiple meanings of words, or of similar-sounding words, for an intended humorous or rhetorical effect. Here are three examples of puns. The pun (word with the double meaning) is in italics.

1. He has been a jogger for three years *running.*

2. An electrician's work is well *grounded.*

3. He had a difficult time *bouncing* back from his bungee-cord accident.

In this brain challenge, you will be given a sentence and asked to fill in the pun. The puzzle title provides a clue to the pun.

TIMED PLAY:

To create a baseline of your processing speed for this puzzle type, time how long it takes you to complete Sets 1–5. Then time yourself again on the completion of Sets 6–10. Compare your two times. If your final time beats your original time, you've improved your processing speed for this type of mental stretch. Bravo!

SET ONE:

BODY PART

The butcher backed into the meat grinder and got a little _____ in his work.

SET TWO:

BOOTLEGGER

She was only a backwoods whiskey maker, but he loved her _____.

ANSWER KEY

FILL IN THE PUN

Set One: Body Part
behind

Set Two: Bootlegger
still

HOW TO PLAY:
See instructions on page 181.

SET THREE:
MEN'S APPAREL
Two silkworms had a race. They ended up in a _____.

SET FOUR:
HAT TRICK
Two hats were hanging on a hat rack in the hallway. One hat said to the other, "You should stay here. I'll go on _____ _____."

ANSWER KEY

FILL IN THE PUN

Set Three: Men's Apparel
tie

Set Four: Hat Trick
a head

FILL IN THE PUN

HOW TO PLAY:
See instructions on page 181.

SET FIVE:
PUPPY SET
A dog gave birth to puppies on the edge of the road, and a policeman cited her for _____.

SET SIX:
FORWARD & BACK
No matter how much you push the envelope, it'll still be _____.

ANSWER KEY

FILL IN THE PUN

Set Five Puppy Set

littering

Set Six: Forward & Back

stationary

FILL IN THE PUN

HOW TO PLAY:
See instructions on page 181.

SET SEVEN:
WATCH OUT!
I wondered why the baseball kept getting bigger and bigger;
then it _____ me.

SET EIGHT:
CURIOSITY
A hole has been found in the nudist-camp wall. The police
are _____ _____ _____.

ANSWER KEY

FILL IN THE PUN

Set Seven: Watch Out!
hit

Set Eight: Curiosity
looking into it

FILL IN THE PUN

HOW TO PLAY:
See instructions on page 181.

SET NINE:
HOLDING BACK
A small boy swallowed some coins and was taken to the hospital.
When his grandmother called and asked the nurse how he was doing,
she replied, "_____ _____ yet."

SET TEN:
DOUBLE NO
A sign on the lawn of a drug-rehab center said: "Keep off the
_____."

ANSWER KEY

FILL IN THE PUN

Set Nine: Holding Back
No change

Set Ten: Double No
grass

ACKNOWLEDGMENTS

I want to thank the following people who made this book possible — from Sellers: Publishing Director Robin Haywood; Editor-in-Chief Mark Chimsky, Managing Editor Mary Baldwin, and Production Editor Charlotte Cromwell; as well as proofreader Renee Rooks Cooley; book designer George Corsillo, Design Monsters; my agent, Coleen O'Shea, Allen O'Shea Literary Agency; Dr. Francis M. Crinella, neuropsychology contributor; and designer Bill Becker, BCGraphicsFL. I would also like to thank my friends and family for their continued support and encouragement.

— *Corinne L. Gediman*

ABOUT THE AUTHORS

Corinne Lille Gediman

Corinne Lille Gediman is a learning and development consultant with 25 years of experience designing and facilitating learning opportunities for corporate clients around the globe. Currently she is applying her skills as an adult learning specialist to the field of neuropsychology. In partnership with Dr. Francis M. Crinella, a clinical neuropsychologist and researcher at UC Irvine, she has authored two previous books on brain fitness including: *Brainfit: 10 Minutes a Day for a Sharper Mind and Memory* (Rutledge Hill Press) and *Supercharge Your Memory!* (Sterling Press). She hosts a Web site on brain fitness (www.brainfit.net) and is a sought-after speaker on radio, television, and destination spas.

Francis M. Crinella, Ph.D.

Dr. Francis Michael Crinella is the Director of the Neuropsychology Laboratory and a Clinical Professor of Neuropsychology at the University of California at Irvine. Dr. Crinella is a highly respected neuropsychologist who has devoted his career to the study of brain function and brain plasticity. In addition to teaching and his clinical practice, Dr. Crinella has conducted numerous research studies and written many academic papers on brain plasticity, memory, and mental agility.